WIND SAYS

WIND SAYS
风在说

Selected Poetry of
Bai Hua
柏桦

Translated from Chinese by Fiona Sze-Lorrain

Zephyr Press & The Chinese University Press of Hong Kong
Brookline, Mass | Hong Kong

Cover image by Xu Bing
Book design by *type*slowly
Printed in Hong Kong

Some of these poems first appeared in *Bitter Oleander, Brooklyn Rail (InTranslation),
Cerise Press, Chutzpah, Mānoa*, and *Poetry Salzburg Review*.

This publication is supported by the Jintian Literary Foundation. Zephyr Press
also acknowledges with gratitude the financial support of the
Massachusetts Cultural Council.

massculturalcouncil.org

Zephyr Press, a non-profit arts and education 501(c)(3) organization,
publishes literary titles that foster a deeper understanding of cultures
and languages. Zephyr Press books are distributed to the trade in the U.S.
and Canada by Consortium Book Sales and Distribution [www.cbsd.com]
and by Small Press Distribution [www.spdbooks.org].

Published for the rest of the world by:
The Chinese University Press
The Chinese University of Hong Kong
Sha Tin, N.T., Hong Kong

Cataloguing-in publication data is available from the Library of Congress.

ZEPHYR PRESS
www.zephyrpress.org

JINTIAN
www.jintian.net

THE CHINESE UNIVERSITY PRESS
www.chineseupress.com

CONTENTS

(VIII) *Character Sketches*

A Prelude to Bai Hua's Lyricism

Fiona Sze-Lorrain

> And to finish: I remember only
> that there was mist. And whoever
> remembers only mist —
> what does he remember?
>
> — Yehuda Amichai, "Letter"

What is lyricism but a walk — an authenticating act of memory — for contemporary Chinese poet Bai Hua? From season to season, he returns to summer in both meditative lyrics and sharply focused vignettes that anchor specific narratives in his poems. Time lost its shoes, meditates Neruda. In a similar manner, Bai Hua's engagement with summer is a timeless experience which moves through events and dramas re-enacted in writings created at different phases of his life. "Sea Summer," "Goodbye, Summer," "Summer Is Still Far," "Mass Summer," "Summer Read: Biography of a Poet," "Summer, 1966," "Summer Lyric" . . . Why summer — this curiosity opens to larger questions, embedded in a reservoir of autobiographical details, impressions, emotional underpinnings, objects, animals, *dramatis personae,* muses and musings from the poet's world. Summer is Bai Hua's weather for poetry. In a mix of chagrin, old griefs and nostalgic yearnings, he often renews the season as both event and metaphor. A repository of public meanings and collective acts, summer as a sustained projection of Bai Hua's poetic imagination also centers on intimate moments, ironies, recklessness, and desires.

For Balzac, "That rose, like all roses, only bloomed for one morning." For Bai Hua who asks if summer is far, "That summer, like all summers, only bloomed for one life."

Drawing, thinking, speaking and ministering — Bai Hua explores language as a multi-dimensional medium in which image and voices mold words and synergies into portraits and encounters. Consider "Character Sketches," for example. Any narrative movement that takes place in this sequence of "portrait poems" is patterned rather than plotted. The poet's so-called experimental work appears to have begun with "Hand Notes on Mountain and Water," in which he cites sources from Mao Tse-tung and *The Pillow Book*, while inserting anecdotes, riddle-like observations and travel notes. Bai Hua took two years to complete this quirky poem of twenty-seven odd fragments. I read it as an ancient form of the Japanese *zuihitsu*, which literally means "follow the brush" — random jottings at specific moments.

★ ★ ★

The strangeness of litany, rhythm and incantation in many tongues inhabit a space the poet later called a "hybrid work," poems in open dialogue with other texts. In her study on Bakhtin and carnival, French linguistic theorist and psychoanalyst Julia Kristeva defines this concept as "intertextuality." With its mosaic of references and quotes in synchronic and diachronic modes, the materiality of the language fabric in Bai Hua's recent work can only thicken. More than bearing mere emotional weight, it is as much a palimpsest as a collage of competing and superimposed textual intensities. Verses remain wakeful amidst interchanging tenses and pronoun references within one narrative thread. I am looking at "Curtain Call" and "Wind Says." The "I" is a construct while "you" and "he" interrupt the habit of rhetorical agreement, creating a new reading gaze at each turn. Writing, unlike reading, is no longer obedient to a linear progression. At the same time we read Bai Hua's poetry, his poetry is reading us.

★ ★ ★

Yesterday, an email arrived from Bai Hua — *Can you please remember to date the poems?*

⋆ ⋆ ⋆

On the affections and disaffections of landscape, Bai Hua turns to Jiangnan. In Nature and its goodness, he has found a governing vision of transcendence, and a sense of place that further expands the largesse of a poetic self: "Is sentimentality too empty? / Which sadness is sadness? / O, thin, tired man / Look, a spring river is flowing east" ("A View of Jiangnan").

Unlike traditional pastoral poets and landscape artists, Bai Hua does not depict thriving or romantic representations of the landscape. The literal world within and without, here run the undercurrents of poetry. There is neither pastoral contentment nor dramatic exile in Bai Hua's work. Rather, Jiangnan scenery serves as a sanctuary for him to anchor or re-appropriate his poetic existence, perhaps even to attain newer potentials for self-realization. The word "nature" derives its meaning from the Latin *nascor*: to grow, to arise, to be born. "Two Days in Huangshan" makes a silent claim for an internal and circular odyssey, as opposed to defining a terminal destination. After all, even the poet himself "tumbles from the landscape." Why then seek Jiangnan when it can't be the guide? Perhaps he is delving into a journey in Jiangnan the same way as Wordsworth had "escaped / from the vast city":

> I look about, and should the guide I choose
> Be nothing better than a wandering cloud,
> I cannot miss my way.

⋆ ⋆ ⋆

How much democracy must I exercise between translating words and translating their distance? Translation isn't always a love affair. The porosity of recurring words or images perceived as important "carriers of lyricism" — "beautiful," "tears," "dusk" and "darkness," for instance — calls for clandestine readings of what may come across as ideologically driven or convenient in the source language. Is the adjective "beautiful" just "beautiful"? Is "dusk" a uniform metaphor in different cultural modes? How can I allow the outburst to startle, the image to leap in its "language of destination"? Some of Bai Hua's early poems are non-discursive and music-derived. Can my translation better cherish the alliteration and the yell that are otherwise audible in its source language? How can the feel stay sensual without being indulgent? Have I honored silence?

Cadences distinguish poetry from prose. The former can sing, the latter must hold. While his new poems require a greater degree of intellectual collaboration than say, those written during the eighties, almost all of Bai Hua's work is markedly rhythmic and incantatory. They contain velocities, says the poet. Yet to compose/transpose a real music also means to confront the authority (or can I be honest — occasional tyranny?) of the Chinese language.

★ ★ ★

This compilation, *Wind Says*, comes to completion in one French summer. A temporal accident, it is probably not pure coincidence.

★ ★ ★

Many thought his representative work, "Summer Is Still Far," was a love poem. "It isn't," says the poet. "It is an elegy for my father, an affectionate reverie of our times together. Our little bamboo house, his white shirt . . ." Far from being a mere resuscitator of the past, this key poem shapes and performs the close proximity of the speaking voice to the identity of the poet himself. The "speaker" floats in aria. Because of its restlessness, the "self" that does not always masquerade as "I" works both inside and outside the poem. Narrative and lyric blend at odds when something else is at stake. I ask who the hero is.

★ ★ ★

In a bowl of air and parsed colors. Cities fallen to the status of verbs. Chongqing, Nanjing, Guangzhou and Chengdu.

★ ★ ★

While working on "In the Qing Dynasty" and "Cloud Diviner," I came across a review essay entitled "Toward a Writerly Poetry" by Chinese critic and poet, Zang Di. A seminal study that situates post-Misty poets in the historical context of the modern Chinese poetry, it first appeared in 1993, a time when most attention was still centered around the Misty poetry aesthetics. In his observations about post-Misty poetry, Zang Di cited Bai Hua's work:

> On the subject of writing, post-Misty poets are conscious that, in all likelihood, they will never reach consensus on the issues of tradition and criticism. For this reason, they have adopted a nihilistic attitude in public, but in their writing they are in fact able to clearly delineate the tradition they face. (. . .)

> In Roland Barthes' words, as cited by Todorov: outstanding poetry is "that which possesses superior expression without entering the personal . . . It is secret while being open." Based on this criterion, two important post-Misty

poets are exemplary: Bai Hua and Zhai Yongming. They display a genius in handling the relationship between the special characteristic of the tradition without antecedents of writing modern poetry and traditional poetry. Their writing is not simply a product of a consciousness of style but manifests an even greater comprehension of the essence of modern poetry.

★ ★ ★

In his early twenties, Bai Hua felt enlightened by Baudelaire, who declared that Nature is a temple, and that any perceived world is a metaphor for the self. He read T.S. Eliot and Mandelstam voraciously, and saw poetry as a sacred duty. *If a poet is indeed a priest, a seer, am I as courageous as Mandelstam?* Conflicted with this question when working overnight on "To Osip Mandelstam," Bai Hua came close to a heartbreaking but earnest *I am not.*

★ ★ ★

Is summer far, as if free.
Once a memory this among many, wind gathers, a swallow
    will return.

*Paris, July 2010**

* The translator wishes to thank Maryanne Hannan and Sally Molini for their wisdom, and Christopher Mattison for his patience and precision in working on this book.

WIND SAYS
风在说

(I) *Precipice*

海的夏天

该是怎样一个充满老虎的夏天
火红的头发被目光唤醒
飞翔的匕首刺伤寂寞的沙滩
急速而老练的海湾怒吼着
举起深深的鲜花
迎接奔跑的阿拉伯少年

有毒的舌头和燃烧的荆棘
包围了广大的火焰
瘦小的结石般的心
溶化鲸鱼、嘴唇和浪潮

叛逆的动乱的儿子
空气淹死了你的喘气和梳子
你的笨拙的头发和感情

黄昏的情调，血的情调
精致的破坏，任意的破坏
蜜蜂和白鸟领着道路
去眩晕
去孤独地埋葬浩瀚

黑暗的洞穴和指尖
将熄灭你的青春和梦想
将杀害你阴险的岁月和勇敢

是怎样的舌尖舔你
怎样的大炮轰你
一支小翅膀或万支箭羽

Sea Summer

What tigerful summer should it be
Fiery hair awakened by a gaze
Flying daggers pierce the lonely beach
Swift and seasoned, the sea howls
holds flowers from down deep
welcomes a running Arabian youth

Poisonous tongue, burning thistles
ambush a vast fire
Thin and small stone hearts
melt whales, lips and waves

Rebellious and riotous son
air drowns your breath, your comb
your clumsy hair and emotions

Mood of dusk, feel of blood
destroy finely, destroy wilfully
Bees and white birds lead the way
vertiginous
bury immensity in solitude

Dark caves and fingertips
will extinguish your youth and dreams
will murder your sinister years and valor

What tongue-tip licks you
What cannon strikes you
A small wing or ten thousand vanes

晶莹的泪花打开
钥匙、美人鱼、纤细的流浪儿
以及整个黎明的灿烂无比

愤慨的夏天
有着狷介的狂躁和敏感
愁绪若高山、若钟楼

历史和头颅熊熊崩坍
是谁在警告，在焚烧，在摧毁
海的短暂的夏天

1984年3月

Sparkling tears open
keys, mermaids, slim wanderers
and the entire splendor of dawn

Indignant summer
has righteous mania and sensitivity
Melancholy like mountains and clocktowers

History and skulls fall in flames
Who is warning, burning and wrecking
impermanent sea summer

March 1984

或别的东西

钉子在漆黑的边缘突破
欲飞的瞳孔及门
暗示一次方向的冲动
可以是一个巨大的毛孔
一束倒立的头发
一块典雅的皮肤
或温暖的打字机的声音
也可以是一柄镶边小刀
一片精致的烈火
一枝勃起的茶花
或危险的初夏的堕落

娇小的玫瑰与乌云进入同一呼吸
延伸到月光下的凉台
和树梢的契机
沉着地注视
无垠的心跳的走廊
正等待
亲吻、拥抱、掐死
雪白的潜伏的小手
以及风中送来的抖颤的苹果

被害死的影子
变成阴郁的袖口
贴紧你
充满珍贵的死亡的麝香
化为红色的嘴唇
粘着你
青苔的气氛使你的鼻子眩晕，下坠

Or Something Else

A nail breaks through the edge of darkness
the pupil of an eye a door wants to fly
hinting at an impulsive direction
perhaps a huge pore
a tuft of hair standing on end
a patch of fine skin
or a typewriter's warm voice
could also be a flange knife
an elegant flame
a sprouting camellia
or the perilous descent of early summer

The petite rose and the dark cloud fuse as one breath
stretch to the moonlit balcony
and the juncture of treetop
staring calmly
the boundless corridors of heartbeat
awaiting
kisses, hugs, strangulation
a small white hand in ambush
and a trembling apple from the wind

The slain shadow
becomes a forlorn sleeve cuff
it sticks tight to you
filled with death's precious musk
melting into red lips
it glues onto you
a mossy feel, your giddy nose droops

此刻你用肃穆切开子夜
用膝盖粉碎回忆
你所有热烈的信心与胆怯
化为烟雾
水波
季节
或老虎

1984年5月

At this instant you slice open night with solemnity
smash memory with a knee
all your fervent confidence and fear
turns into smoke
a wave
a season
or a tiger

May 1984

再见，夏天

我用整个夏天同你告别
我的悲怆和诗歌
皱纹劈啪点起
岁月在焚烧中变为勇敢的痛哭

泪水汹涌，燃遍道路
燕子南来北去
证明我们苦难的爱情
暴雨后的坚贞不屈

风迎面扑来，树林倾倒
我散步穿过黑色的草地
穿过干枯的水库
心跳迅速，无言而感动

我来向你告别，夏天
我的痛苦和幸福
曾火热地经历你的温柔
忘却吧、记住吧、再见吧，夏天！

1984年8月

Goodbye, Summer

I use all of summer to bid you farewell
My woes and poems
Wrinkles flash out like lightning
Years become brave tears in fire

A flood of tears, roads burn
Swallows come and go
proving the ordeal of our love
the perseverance after a storm

Wind rushes in, trees fall
I stroll past a dark pasture
past a dry reservoir
silent but moved, my heart beating fast

I come to bid you farewell, summer
My anguish and bliss
once ardently lived your tenderness
Let's forget, let's remember, goodbye summer

August 1984

悬崖

一个城市有一个人
两个城市有一个向度
寂静的外套无声地等待

陌生的旅行
羞怯而无端端地前进
去报答一种气候
克制正杀害时间

夜里别上阁楼
一个地址有一次死亡
那依稀的白颈项
正转过头来

此时你制造一首诗
就等于制造一艘沉船
一棵黑树
或一片雨天的堤岸

忍耐变得莫测
过度的谜语
无法解开的貂蝉的耳朵
意志无缘无故地离开

器官突然枯萎
李贺痛哭
唐代的手再不回来

1984 秋

Precipice

a city, a man
two cities, an orientation
a quiet overcoat awaits in stillness

a strange voyage
shy advances for no reason
to requite a weather
restraint is murdering time

don't go to the attic at night
an address bears a death
that hazy white neck
is turning its head around

you are now creating a poem
like building a sunken boat
a black tree
or a levee in the rain

endurance becomes unfathomable
an excessive riddle
mysterious ears of Diao Chan
willpower exits for no reason

organs shrivel suddenly
Li Ho weeps
hands from the Tang era will never return

Autumn 1984

白头巾

那边有个声音在喊我
准备一次见面
一场突然的哭泣
在深夜
点起两支神秘的香

那边有个声音在喊我
安排一个动机
眼睛死死地盯着
在深夜
点起两支神秘的香

此刻，我俩将创造一个陌生
并属于这个陌生
不会有太多的笑
但我们得承认
有三个夜晚已经死了

1984 冬

White Headscarf

A voice shouts for me
prepares for our first meeting
sudden sobs
late at night
lighting two mysterious incense

A voice shouts for me
arranges a motive
its eyes stare deadly
late at night
lighting two mysterious incense

We both now create a strangeness
and belong to this strangeness
without many smiles
But we must admit
three nights are dead

Winter 1984

(II) *Summer Is Still Far*

夏天还很远

一日逝去又一日
某种东西暗中接近你
坐一坐，走一走
看树叶落了
看小雨下了
看一个人沿街而过
夏天还很远

真快呀，一出生就消失
所有的善在十月的夜晚进来
太美，全不察觉
巨大的宁静如你干净的布鞋
在床边，往事依稀、温婉
如一只旧盒子
一个褪色的书签
夏天还很远

偶然遇见，可能想不起
外面有一点冷
左手也疲倦
暗地里一直往左边
偏僻又深入
那唯一痴痴的挂念
夏天还很远

再不了，动辄发脾气，动辄热爱
拾起从前的坏习惯
灰心年复一年

Summer Is Still Far

Days come and go
something nears you in the dark
Sit a while, walk a little
watch the leaves fall
watch the light rain
and a man crossing a street
Summer is still far

How fast, it vanishes at its birth
All goodness arrives one October night
Too beautiful, beyond notice
Vast serenity like your clean cotton shoes
By the bed, the past feels hazy and mild
like an old box
a faded bookmark
Summer is still far

A chance encounter, I can't quite remember
A little cold outside
my left hand is tired
It keeps sliding to the left in the dark
far yet profound
The one and only silly nostalgia
Summer is still far

No longer quick-tempered or impassioned
you pick up bad habits from the past
disheartened year after year

小竹楼、白衬衫
你是不是正当年？
难得下一次决心
夏天还很远

1984 冬

Little bamboo house, a white shirt
Are you in the prime of life?
For once, a rare resolution
Summer is still far

Winter 1984

三月

月亮无言
一枚徽章无言
极端的春天一寸寸成熟
新的流水代替了旧日的舌头

这时我们需要说明
说明将雨的天空和撤退的鸟群
说明为什么另一种风
如同真理
向我们进攻

沉睡中剩下的忏悔无邪
苦涩的春梦
使我们失去了充沛的骑手
只有盛开的街道
从耳边疾驰
无边的风声在说
还得放弃
还得记住
每一个老人和儿童

1985 春

March

Speechless moon
A speechless badge
The radical spring ripens inch by inch
New running water replaces old tongue

Now we need to clarify
clarify the rainy sky and birds in retreat
clarify why another wind
invades us
like truth

Pure is remorse, the remains of sleep
Bitter spring dreams
deprive us of our ardent riders
Only the street, flourishing
gallops by the ear
a boundless wind that says
you must abandon
you must remember
every old man every child

Spring 1985

下午

焦虑的寂静已经感到
在一本打开的散文里
在一首余音缭绕的歌里
是的，我注意到了
还有更重要的一点
某个人走进又走出

入睡前你一直在沉思
徒劳的镜子凝视着什么
即将切开的水果
或棕色的浅梦

下午你睡得很稳
脾气也成了酒
是的，我注意到了这一切
包括窗帘有一点美丽
你的梦在过渡

这是最好的时间
但要小心
因为危险是不说话的
它像一件事情
像某个人的影子很轻柔
它走进又走出

1985 春

Afternoon

you can feel an anguished stillness
in an open book of prose
in a song that spirals
yes, I notice
something more fatal
a man is walking in and out

before sleep you contemplate
a vain mirror stares
fruits to be sliced
or a brown light dream

you sleep well in the afternoon
even your temper has become wine
yes, I notice all these
even the faint beauty of curtains
your dreams are in transition

this is the best moment
but take care
for danger is silent
like an incident
a shadow, light and soft
it walks in and out

Spring 1985

书

一本书籍里有一切的梦想
你可以把它读作燕子的飞翔
或者读作春天的虎群的跳跃
你可以把自己放进书中央
就像把自己放进一所房间
或者一个随便的城市
让灵气向四处传达
或者撤出来
又重新返回，再不逃亡

无穷的历代的典籍
阿拉伯的数学书
亡灵书，发黄变脆的诗稿
同样会使你想起一次无益的远征
以及一个天才被浪费的危险

其实所有的榜样同一天打开
一本书籍里有一切的梦想

1985 春

Book

A book contains all kinds of dreams
You can read it as the flight of swallows
or the leap of spring tigers
You can place yourself at its center
like in a room
or in any city
channeling inspiration everywhere
Or you can retire
only to return and flee no more

Magnum opus from endless ages
Arabic mathematical books
The Book of the Dead, yellowed manuscripts
remind you of a futile expedition
a danger that wastes away genius

All archetypes actually begin on the same day
A book contains all kinds of dreams

Spring 1985

鱼

难以理解的鱼不会歌唱
从寂静游进寂静

需要东西、需要说话
但却盲目地看着一块石头

忍受的力量太精确
衰老催它走上仁慈的道路

它是什么？一个种族的形象
或一个无声的投入的动作

埋怨的脸向阴影
死亡的沉默向错误

出生为了说明一件事的比喻
那源于暧昧的痛苦的咽喉

1985 秋

30

Fish

Unfathomable, the fish can't sing
swimming from silence to silence

It needs things, it needs to speak
but it stares blindly at a stone

The strength of endurance is too precise
Senility urges it to walk the road of kindness

What is it? Image of a people
or an act of soundless immersion?

The face of grievance veers toward shadow
the silence of death toward error

Born as metaphor to clarify a fact:
the throat where ambiguous pain begins

Autumn 1985

途中

日子从这一页路过
注视受祝福的水果，注视前途
倾听来自另一只耳朵
来自体内的阴影，不灭的气候

忧伤的思绪在途中开满
在一件小东西里发觉又失落
催促多么温柔
精致的钢笔低声倾诉
哦，一群群消失的事物

一幢房子拆了
必要的杯子拿走了
每天都要发生一些事情
但我们仍然这样走着

1985

En Route

Days pass by this page
observe blessed fruits and the future
listen from another ear
inner shadows and unchecked weather

Thoughts of sorrow open midway
a small object is found and lost
such tender coaxing
an exquisite pen murmurs
O, things that vanish batch by batch

A house is demolished
A crucial cup is stolen
A few events must happen every day
Yet we still walk on like this

1985

民国的下午

有一个人在叩门，用忧伤的指头
有一个人在行走，也心事重重
有一个人在叹气，提着个八哥
有一个人在痛苦，浑身发抖
就让他像这副样子吧
谁察觉谁就如释重负

要盼望什么？要说明什么？
注视或忘却即将合拢
心急如焚又藏而不露
寂静暗中包围着
翻飞的树叶正迷离扑朔

那就下定决心吧
让那人反复叩门
让那人反复行走
让那人反复叹气
让那人反复痛苦
你就坐在这里一丝不动

1985

A Republican Afternoon

A man knocks on the door with sad fingers
A man walks with a burdened mind
A man sighs, holding up a mynah bird
A man suffers, trembling from head to toe
Let him be so
Who senses who, what a relief

What is there to hope for? To explain?
Gaze or oblivion will fold
Anxiety hides and veils
Silence ambushes in secret
Leaves sway in the air, an enigma

Make up your mind
Let that man go on knocking
go on walking
go on sighing
go on suffering
you will just sit here, motionless

1985

(III)   *In the Qing Dynasty*

望气的人

望气的人行色匆匆
登高眺远
眼中沉沉的暮霭
长出黄金、几何与宫殿

穷巷西风突变
一个英雄正动身去千里之外
望气的人看到了
他激动的草鞋和布衫

更远的山谷浑然
零落的钟声依稀可闻
两个儿童打扫着亭台
望气的人坐对空寂的傍晚

吉祥之云宽大
一个干枯的导师沉默
独自在吐火、炼丹
望气的人看穿了石头里的图案

乡间的日子风调雨顺
菜田一畦，流水一涧
这边青翠未改
望气的人已走上了另一座山巅

1986 暮春

Cloud Diviner

The cloud diviner scurries by
scanning from heights
In his eyes, the dense dusky mist
grows gold, geometry and palaces

In a poor quarter, the west wind turns abruptly
A hero embarks on a thousand-mile journey
The cloud diviner can see
his agitated grass sandals and toga

Farther valleys merge into one
the chimes of bells, faint and few
Two children are sweeping the pavilions
The cloud diviner faces an empty twilight

Auspicious clouds unfold
A quiet shriveled master
spits fire, brews elixir on his own
The cloud diviner sees patterns in the stones

Wind and rain agree in village days
A vegetable field, a flowing stream
the crispy green stays unchanged here
The cloud diviner has left for the next summit

Late Spring, 1986

李后主

遥远的清朗的男子
在977年一个细瘦的秋天
装满表达和酒
彻夜难眠、内疚
忠贞的泪水在湖面漂流

梦中的小船像一首旧曲
思念挥霍的岁月
负债的烟
失去的爱情的创伤
一个国家的沦落

哦，后主
林阴雨昏、落日楼头
你摸过的栏杆
已变成一首诗的细节或珍珠
你用刀割着酒、割着衣袖
还用小窗的灯火
吹燃竹林的风、书生的抱负
同时也吹燃了一个风流的女巫

1986 暮春

Emperor Li Yu

Long ago a bright man
in the thin autumn of 977
full of lyricism and wine
sleepless and guilty all night
tears of loyalty drifting on the lake

A boat in a dream like an old prelude
recalling wasted years
indebted smoke
wounds of a lost love
a nation's fall

O, Emperor
dark sky and rainy dusk
the handrail you once touched
has turned into pearls or poetic details
you slice wine with a knife, you slice a sleeve
you even use window lights
to blow flames into a bamboo wind, a scholar's ambitions
a flirtatious sorceress

Late Spring, 1986

黄昏

递给我走来的树木
递给我一本历史书
出出进进的死亡受冷落
传达的力量铭心刻骨

心跳穿过缓慢的阴影
随便的一只鸟儿
飞向随便的一片天空
风中有漂泊的路途

肉体日夜流逝
几个名字返老还童
梦中的夏天开始凋零
无声的耳朵倾听一个人物

为了百年如一日
为了此刻天长地久
请递给我走来的树木
递给我一本历史书

1986

Dusk

Give me the forest I have walked through
Give me a book of history
Death comes and goes, isolated
Its power engraved in me

Heartbeat runs through slow shadows
A carefree bird
flies toward a carefree sky
Wind has a wandering path

Flesh fades away day and night
Some names are young again
Summer in dreams begins to wither
A silent ear listens to a personage

To live a century as a day
To eternalize this moment
Please give me the forest I have walked through
Give me a book of history

1986

在清朝

在清朝
安闲和理想越来越深
牛羊无事，百姓下棋
科举也大公无私
货币两地不同
有时还用谷物兑换
茶叶、丝、瓷器

在清朝
山水画臻于完美
纸张泛滥，风筝遍地
灯笼得了要领
一座座庙宇向南
财富似乎过分

在清朝
诗人不事营生、爱面子
饮酒落花，风和日丽
池塘的水很肥
二只鸭子迎风游泳
风马牛不相及

在清朝
一个人梦见一个人
夜读太史公，清晨扫地
而朝廷增设军机处
每年选拔长指甲的官吏

In the Qing Dynasty

In the Qing dynasty
ease and ideals flourish
cows and sheep do nothing, the folks play chess
even imperial exams are fair and selfless
different currencies in two places
sometimes they barter crops
for tea, silk and china

In the Qing dynasty
landscape art defines perfect
a flood of paper, kites everywhere
lanterns lead the way
temples after temples turn southward
even wealth seems over the top

In the Qing dynasty
poets have no trade, save face
drinking over fallen leaves and fine weather
fat pond water
two ducks swim and greet the wind
at complete odds

In the Qing dynasty
a man dreams of a man
reads Sima Qian at night, sweeps the floor in the morning
the court creates more military sites
appoints officers with long nails each year

在清朝
多胡须和无胡须的人
严于身教，不苟言谈
农村人不愿认字
孩子们敬老
母亲屈从于儿子

在清朝
用款税激励人民
办水利、办学校、办祠堂
编印书籍、整理地方志
建筑弄得古香古色

在清朝
哲学如雨，科学不能适应
有一个人朝三暮四
无端端地着急
愤怒成为他毕生的事业
他于一八四二年死去

1986 秋

46

In the Qing dynasty
men with beards and men with no beards
behave strictly, converse little
country folks refuse to read
children respect the old
mothers listen to their sons

In the Qing dynasty
taxes motivate people
build irrigation, schools and temples
print books, classify annals
lend architecture a classical touch

In the Qing dynasty
philosophy is rain, science can't adapt
a fickle-minded man
anxious for no reason
ends his lifelong career in rage
dies in 1842

Autumn 1986

(IV) *Jonestown*

秋天的武器

斗争走向极端
口号走向极端
吃石头的刺刀走向极端
我听到空气的坠落

这完全适合于你
在古代的秋天
一个人因此而死亡
吞下厌烦
吞下纸老虎
而人民的嘴不朝向耳朵

今天我要重新开始
研究各种牺牲
漫天要价的光芒
尖锐的革命的骨头

在此时，在成都
所有的人迎面走来
把汽车给我
把极端给我
把暴力和广场给我

1986 秋

Autumn Weapon

Combat goes to the extreme
Slogan goes to the extreme
Stone-eating knives go to the extreme
I can hear the collapse of air

This suits you perfectly
In ancient autumn
a man died
swallowing ennui
and paper tigers
People shifted their mouths away from their ears

Today I want to start fresh
study every kind of sacrifice
exorbitant radiance
sharp bones of revolution

Right now in Chengdu
all men come forth
to give me cars
to give me the extreme
to give me violence and the square

Autumn 1986

我歌唱生长的骨头

我歌唱生长的骨头
那些庞大的骨头
那些吹动的呼喊的骨头
那些被围住的凄楚的笑

在一个艳阳天
证实了那将死亡的男孩
呵，我的肥胖的厚嘴唇的男孩
我的一枚铜钱
你无用的泪
已冲向一些潮湿的朋友

雨中的步行者，焕发的斜坡
他们挑剔暴力和美貌
但不配分享行礼

家长们在接受茶叶
他们的儿子
那些纯洁的性交者
在今天正午
吟咏药物

呵，一个盲人谈到笑
一个怠于学习的学生当上伪善的父亲
那少汗的体弱的运动家
那堆积如山的食品
拒绝了晚来的客人

Bones from My Singing

Bones from my singing
those massive bones
those stirring, yelling bones
those ambushed tragic smiles

One sunny day
confirms the dying boy
O, my boy with fat, thick lips
my only coin
Your useless tears
have rushed to soggy friends

Strollers in the rain, sparkling slopes
They pick at violence and beauty
do not deserve a share of grace

Parents accept tea leaves
their sons
those pure love-makers
they are reciting medication
this afternoon

Ha, a blind man talks about laughter
a lazy student becomes a hypocritical father
That frail athlete who hardly perspires
That mountain of canned food
rejecting late visitors

而争着冲向我怀中的
是人类的病症
热的摄取者

通通经过这一天
这一天
我们的形象得以统一

1987 春

Rushing to my arms
an illness of mankind
Hot profiteers

all pass by this day
This day
our image is unified

Spring 1987

群众的夏天

自从我们脱离了冬天
烧着的词典燃痛了鱼群
美的本质被抽象的钥匙打开
生命正热闹、搁置

亲戚在翻窗入户
频繁的老人努力生活
身边的树木已经送走
送进异乡人的嘴里

盛大的食品、热的节日
涌进胃的窄门
发疯的空气辗转反侧
肉体承担了寒冷的衬衣

由于精神的匮乏
我们接受了物质的教训
熟透的铁、花之汗
在普遍的胳膊里流行

当风吹亮一些绸缎
男孩彻底地软了
城市开始没有群众
真实的中央，群众争度夏天

1987年8月

Mass Summer

since we separated from winter
a burning dictionary scalded shoals of fish
an abstract key opened the essence of beauty
life was hectic and cast aside

kinsmen sneaked in through windows
old men were working hard all the time
trees by the side had sent away
into foreign mouths

lavish food, popular festivals
into the narrow gate of a stomach
mad air tossed and turned
flesh took on a cold shirt

because of spiritual poverty
we took lessons from materialism
ripe iron and sweat of flowers
prevailed in common arms

when wind lit up silk
boys softened fully
soon, the city had no mass
a true center, masses fight for summer

August 1987

献给曼杰斯塔姆

那个生活在神经里的人
害怕什么呢？
害怕赤身裸体的纯洁？
不！害怕声音
那甩掉了思想的声音

我梦想中的诗人
穿过太重的北方
穿过瘦弱的幻觉的童年
你难免来到人间

今天，我承担你怪僻的一天
今天，我承担你天真的一天
今天，我突出你的悲剧

沉默在指明
诗篇在心跳、在怜惜
无辜的舌头染上语言
这也是我记忆中的某一天

牛已经停止耕耘
镰刀已放弃亡命
风正屏住呼吸
啊，寒冷，你在加紧运送冬天

焦急的莫斯科
你握紧了动人的肺腑
迎着漫天雪花、翘首以待
啊，你看，他来了

To Osip Mandelstam

What does the man who lives in folly
fear?
The purity of a naked body?
No! Voices —
voices free of thoughts

My dream poet
travels through the heavy north
the weak illusory childhood
You can't help but arrive in this world

Today I'll bear your eccentricity
shoulder your innocence
heighten your tragedy

Silence points out —
The heart of poetry is beating, lamenting
An innocent tongue is dyed with language
This is also a memorable day

Cows have stopped plowing
Sickles have quit toiling
Wind holds its breath
O cold, you hasten to drive winter away

Anxious Moscow
you tighten your poignant organs
waiting before the snowy sky
Ah, look, he is here

我们诗人中最可泣的亡魂！
他正朝我走来

我开始属于这儿
我开始钻进你的形体
我开始代替你残酷的天堂
我，一个外来的长不大的孩子
对于这一切
路边的群众只能更孤单

1987年11月

The most tragic ghost among us poets!
He is walking toward me

I begin to belong here
to enter your body
to replace your cruel heaven
I — a foreign child who never grows up
In the face of these
roadside masses feel only lonelier

November 1987

美人

我听见孤独的鱼
燃红恭敬的街道
是否有武装上膛的声音
当然还有马群踏弯空气

必须向我致敬，美的行刑队
死亡已整队完毕
开始从深山涌进城里

而一些颜色
一些伪装的沉重与神圣
从我们肉中碎身

衰老的雷管定时于夜半的腹部
孩子们在食物中寻找颓废
年青人由于形象走向斗争

此时谁在吹
谁就是火
谁就是开花的痉挛的脉搏

我指甲上的幽魂，攀登的器官
在酒中成长
雨不停地敲响我们的脑壳

啊，挑剔的气候，心之森林
推动着检阅着泪水
时光的泥塑造我们的骨头

Beauty

I hear solitary fish
blazing humble streets red
is it the sound of arms being loaded
horses curve air with their hoofs

salute me, beautiful fire squads
death has already arrayed itself
pours into the city from mountains

some colors
some pretentious gravity and grandeur
smash into pieces in our flesh

aging detonators are timed for midnight bellies
children seek decadence in food
youths go to battle from an image

who blows now
who is fire
who is the convulsing arm of a new flower

spirits on my fingernails, ascending organs
grown in wine
knock ceaselessly on our skulls

O, picky weather, the forest of heart
propel and inspect tears
the mud of time shapes our bones

整整一个秋天，美人
我目睹了你
你驱赶了、淹死了
我们清洁的上升的热血

1987年11月

one whole summer, beauty
I have witnessed you
you drive away, drown
our clean and rising hot blood

November 1987

琼斯敦

孩子们可以开始了
这革命的一夜
来世的一夜
人民圣殿的一夜
摇撼的风暴的中心
已厌倦了那些不死者
正急着把我们带向那边

幻想中的敌人
穿梭般地袭击我们
我们的公社如同斯大林格勒
空中充满纳粹的气味

热血旋涡的一刻到了
感情在冲破
指头在戳入
胶水广泛地投向阶级
妄想的耐心与反动作斗争

从春季到秋季
性急与失望四处蔓延
示威的牙齿啃着难捱的时日
男孩们胸中的军火渴望爆炸
孤僻的禁忌撕咬着眼泪
看那残食的群众已经发动

一个女孩在演习自杀
她因疯狂而趋于激烈的秀发
多么亲切地披在无助的肩上

Jonestown

children can now begin
this night of revolution
a night of the afterlife
and the people's palace
the convulsive center of a storm
weary of the undying
eager to send us to death

an imaginary enemy
attacks us like air shuttles
our commune stands like Stalingrad
its air smells of the Nazis

the whirlpool of hot blood has arrived
emotions are breaking
fingers jabbing
glue shot into social classes
the patience of vanity battles with counteraction

from spring to fall
impatience and disappointment spreads
the teeth of demonstrations chew on hard times
boys yearn for explosion in their munitions chest
solitary taboos rip tears apart
look, the voracious mob is unleashed

a girl rehearses suicide
her beautiful hair agitated from madness
so tenderly on her helpless shoulders

那是十七岁的标志
唯一的标志

而我们精神上初恋的象征
我们那白得炫目的父亲
幸福的子弹击中他的太阳穴
他天真的亡灵仍在倾注：
信仰治疗、宗教武士道
秀丽的政变的躯体

如山的尸首已停止排演
空前的寂静高声宣誓：
渡过危机
操练思想
纯洁牺牲

面对这集中肉体背叛的白夜
这人性中最后的白夜
我知道这也是我痛苦的丰收夜

1987年12月

an emblem of being seventeen
the only emblem

the spiritual symbol of our first love
our dazzling white father
blissful bullets hit his temples
his naive spirit is still showering
a religion cure, *bushido*
the beautiful body of a *coup d'état*

mountains of corpses have stopped rehearsing
make a loud oath in the stillness:
Outlive the crisis
Drill your thoughts
Purify sacrifice

in this white night that gathers betrayal in flesh
the last white night of humanity
I know, also my painful harvest night

December 1987

恨

这恨的气味是肥肉的气味
也是两排肋骨的气味
它源于意识形态的平胸
也源于阶级的毛多症

我碰见了她，这个全身长恨的人
她穿着惨淡的政治武装
一脸变性术的世界观
三年来除了磕头就神经涣散

这非人的魂魄疯了吗？
这沉湎于斗争的红色娘子军
看她正起义，从肉体直到喘气
直到牙齿浸满盲目的毒汁

一个只为恨而活着的人
一个烈火烧肺的可怜人
她已来到我们中间
她开始了对人类的深仇大恨

1987

Hatred

This hatred smells like fatty meat
and two chunks of rib
It springs from the flat breasts of ideology
from the hirsutism of social class

I've seen her — a woman full of hatred
who wears a bleak political uniform
her sexually transformed face and worldly outlook
dispirited from three years of kowtowing

Is this inhuman soul mad?
Indulged in power, the Red Detachment of Women
stages an uprising from flesh to breath
until blind venom drips from their teeth

A woman who lives for hatred
A pathetic woman whose lungs burn
She is already among us
waging her war of hatred

1987

这寒冷值得纪念

一场大雪接着又一场大雪
漫无目标的冬天啊!
多少个我所熟悉的冬天!
在重庆，在歌乐山

一条铁路在风景中蜿蜒
回忆中的铁路啊
交叉着记忆，交叉着冬天

什么东西在接近我们
什么东西直到说出的那一天
当重复的工作令人生厌

冬天啊，冬天
让孩子去哭吧
让心伤透吧
生活的经济学已达到极限

1987 冬

This Harsh Cold Is Worth Commemorating

A heavy snow after a heavy snow
O, aimless winter
How many winters do I know so well
In Chongqing, in Gele Mountain

A railroad weaves through the scenery
O, railroad of the past
intersecting memories, intersecting winter

What nears us
What once spoken
bores us like tedious work

Winter, O winter
Let the child cry
Let the heart be sad
The economics of life has reached its ends

Winter 1987

(V) *Memories*

往事

这些无辜的使者
她们平凡地穿着夏天的衣服
坐在这里，我的身旁
向我微笑
向我微露老年的害羞的乳房

那曾经多么热烈的旅途
那无知的疲乏
都停在这陌生的一刻
这善意的，令人哭泣的一刻

老年，如此多的鞠躬
本地普通话〔是否必要呢？〕
温柔的色情的假牙
一腔烈火

我已集中精力看到了
中午的清风
它吹拂相遇的眼神
这伤感
这坦开的仁慈
这纯属旧时代的风流韵事

啊，这些无辜的使者
她们频频走动
悄悄叩门
满怀恋爱和敬仰
来到我经历太少的人生

1988年10月

Remembrance

These innocent messengers
wearing plain summer clothes
sitting here, by my side
smiling at me
subtly reveal their old, shy breasts

That once ardent voyage
that ignorant fatigue
all stop in this foreign moment
a kindly teary moment

Age, so much obeisance
local Mandarin   (is it necessary?)
tender and lustful dentures
a gust of fire

I concentrate my energies, can see
the afternoon breeze
blowing across gazes that meet
Such melancholy
such frank benevolence
romantic gaieties of old times

Ah, these innocent messengers
ceaseless, on the move
coyly knocking on the door
harboring love and admiration
arriving in my life of so few experiences

October 1988

回忆

我在初春的阳台上回忆
一九八六年春夜
我和你漫步这幽静的街头
直到天色将明

我在幻想着未来吧
我在对你读一首诗吧
我松开的发辫显得多无力
风吹热我惊慌的脸庞
这脸，这微倦的暖人风光

回忆中无用的白银啊
轻柔的无辜的命运啊
这又一年白色的春夜
我决定自暴自弃
我决定远走他乡

1989年3月

Memories

On a balcony in early spring I recall
a spring night in 1986
walking with you on this quiet street
till daybreak

I was dreaming of the future
I was reciting you a poem
My loosened hair plaits seemed so feeble
Wind warmed my frightened face
This face, a tired warm scene

Useless silver in memories
innocent soft fate
white spring night of yet another year
I decided to give myself up
I decided to break free

March 1989

骑手

冲过初春的寒意
一匹马在暮色中奔驰
一匹马来自冬天的俄罗斯

春风释怀，落木开道
一曲音乐响彻大地
冲锋的骑手是一位英俊少女

七十二小时，已经七十二小时
她激情的加速度
仍以死亡的加速度前进

是什么呼声叩击着中国的原野
是什么呼声象闪电从两边退去
啊，那是发自耳边的沙沙的爱情

命运也测不出这伟大的谜底
太远了，一匹马的命运
太远了，一个孩子的命运

1989 春

Rider

Dashing through the early spring cold
a horse races in dusk
a horse from Russia in winter

Spring wind opens its heart, fallen trees open the way
a melody resonates in the world
The rider in the lead is a beautiful girl

Seventy-two hours, already seventy-two
She accelerates with passion
advances at the acceleration of death

What cry strikes the Chinese pastures
What cry retreats from both ends like lightning
Ah, it is love shuffling by the ear

Even fate can't fathom this grand riddle
The fate of a horse is too far
The fate of a child is too far

Spring 1989

望江南

抒情的人在旷野中
他迎接着、关怀着、树起着
——那春天的形象

抒情的人手拿一把木梳
一把热烈的木梳
他明亮的头发在阳光下闪烁

人们在春天的大地梦游
梅花开满羞怯的山坡
而你，江南游子
一人单独双眉紧锁

缠绵是否太空？
万种闲愁会是哪一种？
啊，细瘦的人儿，疲乏的人儿
你看一江春水向东流

1989年3月

A View of Jiangnan

A lyrical man stands open in the field
welcoming, tending, planting
the image of spring

He holds a wooden comb in his hand
an impassioned comb
His bright hair shines in the sun

Men sleepwalk in the land of spring
Plum blossoms flourish on shy hills
Wanderer of Jiangnan
you knot your eyebrows in loneliness

Is sentimentality too empty?
Which sadness is sadness?
O, thin, tired man
Look, a spring river is flowing east

March 1989

夏日读诗人传记

这哲学令我羞愧
他期望太高
两次打算放弃
不！两次打算去死
漫长的三个月是他沉沦的三个月
我漫长的痛苦跟随他
从北京直到重庆

整整三个月，云游的小孤儿
暗中要成为大诗人
他的童年已经结束
他已经十六岁
他反复说
"要么为自己牺牲自己
要么为别人而活着。"
这哲学令我羞愧

他表达的速度太快了
我无法跟上这意义
短暂的夏日翻过第八十九页
瞧，他孤单的颈子开始发炎
在意义中，也在激情中发炎
并在继续下去
这哲学令我羞愧

再瞧，他的身子
多敏感，多难看
太小了，太瘦了
嘴角太平凡了
只有狡黠的眼神肯定了他的力量

Summer Read: Biography of a Poet

This philosophy puts me to shame
His expectations are too high
Twice he planned to give up
No! Twice he planned to die
Three endless months, his three fallen months
My endless suffering follows him
from Beijing to Chongqing

For three months, the wandering orphan
secretly wants to be a great poet
His childhood has ended
He is already sixteen
He keeps saying
Either I sacrifice myself
or live for others
This philosophy puts me to shame

He expresses himself too quickly
I can't follow this meaning
Brief summer days turn over page eighty-nine
Look, his lonely neck inflames
inflames meaning, passion
and it continues
This philosophy puts me to shame

Look again, his body
so sensitive, so ugly
too small, too thin
The corners of his mouth are too plain
Only his sly eyes confirm his strength

但这是不幸的力量
这哲学令我羞愧

其中还有一些绝望的细节
无人问津的两三个细节
梦游的两三个细节
竖着指头的两三个细节
由于一句话而自杀的细节
那是十八岁的一个细节
这惟一的哲学令我羞愧

1989 冬

But this strength is a misfortune
This philosophy puts me to shame

Still some details within to despair
two, three details no one cares
two, three details in sleepwalk
two, three details with thumbs up
detail of a suicide due to a sentence
It is a detail at eighteen
This philosophy puts me to shame

Winter 1989

1966年夏天

成长啊，随风成长
仅仅三天，三天！

一颗心红了
祖国正临街吹响

吹啊，吹，早来的青春
吹绿爱情，也吹绿大地的思想

瞧，政治多么美
夏天穿上了军装

生活啊！欢乐啊！
那最后一枚像章
那自由与怀乡之歌
哦，不！那十岁的无瑕的天堂

1989年12月26日

Summer, 1966

O growing up, growing up with wind
in three days, just three days!

A heart is red
The nation is blowing trumpets in the streets

O blow, blow, early youth
blow love green, blow our thoughts green

Look, how beautiful politics are
Summer puts on an army uniform

Life! Joy!
The last Mao badge
The song of freedom and nostalgia
No! Ten years, perfect heaven

December 26, 1989

十夜 十夜

十夜，连续十夜
秋天在逼近，树叶在转黄
老师在瘦下去啊
我的书，我的身体
啊，我的，我的，我的
我的每一小时，每一秒
我严峻的左眼代替了心跳

十夜，所有沉重的都睡去
十夜，交媾后的青春、豹
江南和江北都睡去

连续十夜，我躺在床上
连续十夜，十夜压迫我的心房

十夜，十夜
十夜的道路瞭望远方
十夜的少年忘记了理想

十夜，十夜
我面带羞愧来到你们中央
垂下双手，恳请你们原谅

十个夜晚，我听到另一种歌唱
十个夜晚，我听到树木
压倒一切的树木
在我命名的天空轰响

1989年9月

90

Ten Nights Ten Nights

Ten nights, ten nights in a row
Autumn is near, leaves turn yellow
your teacher thins away
my books, my body
O, my, my, my
my every hour, every second
my stern left eye ticks in lieu of a heart

Ten nights, all things heavy have gone to sleep
Ten nights, spring and panther after sex
the north and the south all asleep

Ten nights in a row, I lie on my bed
Ten nights in a row, ten nights oppress my heart

Ten nights, ten nights
the journey of ten nights looks afar
the youth of ten nights forgets ideals

Ten nights, ten nights
I bring my shame to your center
both hands down, ask for your forgiveness

Ten nights, I hear another song
Ten nights, I hear trees
crashing on all trees
thundering in the sky I name

September 1989

教育

我传播着你的美名
一个偷吃了三个蛋糕的儿童
一个无法玩掉一个下午的儿童

旧时代的儿童啊
二十年前的蛋糕啊
那是决定我前途的下午
也是我无法玩掉的下午

家长不老，也不能歌唱
忙于说话和保健
并打击儿童的骨头

寂寞中养成挥金如土的儿子
这个注定要歌唱的儿子
但冬天的思想者拒受教育
冬天的思想者只剩下骨头

1989 冬

Education

I'm spreading the word about your reputation —
a child who stole three cakes
a child who couldn't idle away an afternoon

O, child from the olden times
cakes twenty years ago
That afternoon determined my future
an afternoon I couldn't idle away

Parents neither age nor sing
busy chatting, busy with health care
They hit their children's bones

Prodigal son nourished by loneliness
a son destined to sing
a thinker of winter refusing teachings
with only bones remaining

Winter 1989

麦子：纪念海子

麦子，我面对你
我垂下疼痛的双手
麦子，我左胸的一枚像章
我请求你停止疯长！

麦子！麦子！麦子！
北方就要因此而流血
看吧，从安徽直到我手里
直到祖国的中心
一粒精神正飞速传递

是谁发出绝食的命令
麦子！麦子！麦子！
一滴泪打在饥饿的头顶
你率领绝食进入第168个小时

麦子，我们的麦子
啊，麦子，大地的麦子！
长空星辰照耀
南方在肉体中哭泣

请宣告吧！麦子，下一步，下一步！
下一步就是牺牲
下一步不是宴席

1989 冬

Wheat: In Memory of Hai Zi

Sacrifice realizes lofty ideals
making sun and moon in new skies
— Mao Tse-tung

Wheat, I stand before you
I let my sore hands fall
Wheat, a badge pinned on my left chest
I beg you to stop your mad growth!

Wheat! Wheat! Wheat!
There'll be bloodshed in the north
Look, from Anhui province to my hands
all the way to the heart of our nation
a grain of spirit spreads speedily

Who ordered the hunger strike?
Wheat! Wheat! Wheat!
A tear falls on a starving head
You lead the hunger strike into its 168th hour

Wheat, our wheat
O, wheat, wheat of earth!
Stars beam in the vast sky
The south is weeping in flesh and blood

Please declare, wheat, your next move! The next move!
It will be a sacrifice
It won't be a feast

Winter 1989

95

诗人病历

盛夏也黯然神伤
你没有头盔，没有遮阴的草帽
你走进花园，赤裸着冲动

这青年是一个小儿子
这青年扮演刁钻的角色
这青年承认迷惘

唉，你太瘦，太干
善良的风景也帮不上忙
你还得迅速熟悉各种礼貌

受惊的两耳，一张发票
崩溃的肉体的逻辑
全面服从了火热

就放在你眼前吧
一本书或日日夜夜
你的脸已被怀旧选中

疲乏啊，子弹啊
这镜子处罚着敏锐
这一切难以弥补

你准备向什么挑战
列车飞驰，服装日新月异
生与死只隔一步

The Poet's Medical Record

Even high summer is forlorn
You have no helmet, no straw hat for shade
You walk into the garden, naked and impulsive

This young man is a young son
This young man plays a cunning role
This young man confesses to confusion

Sigh, you are too thin, too dry
Even the kind-hearted scenery cannot help
You must quickly acquaint yourself with all formality

Startled ears, an invoice
The logic of collapsed flesh
obeys fervor entirely

Just put it before your eyes
a book or days and nights
Your face is chosen by nostalgia

Ah fatigue, ah bullet
This mirror punishes shrewdness
All these hardly speak of atonement

You prepare for some challenge
Trains speed past, clothes change fast
Just one step between life and death

你就是沙漠之子
失血、缺水、怀乡
你就是一个技工
在沙上建筑你的语言之墓

1990

You are the son of a desert
hemorrhagic, dehydrated, nostalgic
You are a technician
building your tomb of language in sand

1990

生活

生活，你多么宽广，像道路
带着政权的气味赶往远方

远方，各族人民在歌唱
大嘴唇、尖声音，加上蓝天和广场

广场呀，生长着漫长而颓唐的农业
饕餮或饥饿在四季里彷徨

一切皆遥远，一切皆无关
热情的自身，死的自身，生活的自身

像一个小孤儿独坐大地
像缺乏营养的云，像啊……

像生活，干脆就剥竹、毁稻、杀猪
像生活，干脆就在睡眠中，在睡眠中清账

1990年9月30日

Life

Life, so spacious, like a road
rushing to a distant land with political might

Afar, all men sing
big lips, sharp voices, with blue sky and a square

O square, where endless and failed agriculture grows
gluttons or hunger loiters in four seasons

Everything so far and insignificant
the essence of zest, death and life

Like an orphan sitting on a vast land
or an underfed cloud . . .

Like life, let's just peel bamboo, burn crops and kill pigs
Let's just settle all scores in sleep, in sleep

September 30, 1990

(VI) *The Man Clothed in Birch Bark*

演春与种梨

一

日暮，灯火初上
二人在园里谈论春色
一片黑暗，淙淙水响
呵，几点星光
生活开始了……

暮春，我们聚首的日子
家有春椅、春桌、春酒
呵，纸，纸，纸啊
你沦入写作
并暂时忘记了……

二

足寒伤神，园庭荒凉
他的晚年急于种梨

种梨、种梨
陌生的、温润的梨呀

光阴的梨、流逝的梨
来到他悲剧的正面像

梨的命运是美丽的
他的注视是腼腆的

Performing Spring, Growing Pears

1

Dusk, above the lights
two men are discussing spring in a garden
Darkness, the gurgling of water
Ah, dots of starlight
life has begun . . .

Late spring, the days of our reunion
Spring chair, spring table, spring wine at home
Ah, paper, paper, paper
you sink into writing
forget for now . . .

2

Cold feet and a forlorn look, the gardens, deserted
He is eager to grow pears in his twilight years

Grow pears, grow pears
Strange, moist pears

Pears of time, pears that die
in the full portrait of his tragedy

The destiny of a pear is beautiful
His gaze is shy

但如果生活中没有梨
如果梨的青春会老死

如果、如果……
那他就没有依傍，就不能歌唱

1990年9月30日

But if life has no pear
if the youth of pears dies

If, if . . .
he would have no reliance, he would not sing

September 30, 1990

现实

这是温和，不是温和的修辞学
这是厌烦，厌烦本身

呵，前途、阅读、转身
一切都是慢的

长夜里，收割并非出自必要
长夜里，速度应该省掉

而冬天也可能正是夏天
而鲁迅也可能正是林语堂

1990年12月11日

Reality

This is gentle, an ungentle rhetoric
This is vexing, vexation itself

Ah, future, reading, turn back
all is slow

In a long night, harvest is not essential
In a long night, speed should be abolished

Winter could also be summer
Lu Xun could also be Lin Yutang

December 11, 1990

以桦皮为衣的人

这是纤细的下午四点
他老了

秋天的九月，天高气清
厨房安静
他流下伤心的鼻血

他决定去五台山
那意思是不要捉死蛇
那意思是作诗：

"雪中狮子骑来看"

1990年12月11日

The Man Clothed in Birch Bark

A slender four p.m.
He is old

Autumn in September, clear sky and fresh air
The kitchen is quiet
Sadness bleeds from his nose

He decides to go to Mount Wutai —
Do not catch a dead snake
Write poetry:

Come ride on the snow lion

December 11, 1990

未来

这漂泊物应该回去
寂寞已伤了他的身子

不幸的肝沉湎于鱼与骄傲
不幸的青春加上正哭的酒精

啊，愤怒还需要更大吗？
骂人还骂得不够

鸟、兽、花、木，春、夏、秋、冬
俱惊异于他是一个小疯子

红更红，白更白
黄上加黄，他是他未来的尸体

1990年12月

The Future

The wanderer must return
loneliness has already hurt his body

His ill-fated liver indulged in fish and pride
An ill-fated youth and weeping alcohol

Ah, must you need more rage
aren't your curses enough?

Bird, beast, flower, wood, spring, summer, autumn, winter
astonished that he is a little madman

Red more red, white more white
yellow more yellow, he is the corpse of his future

December 1990

初春

啊，来了，哈哈大笑的春天来了
那牢底已坐穿

再过三天就放学
那翅膀硬了的鸟可以飞了

孩子们在打着包裹
孩子们用手勾画长征的道路

而其中一个孩子举着羊头痛哭
他吵着要穿一件夏天的衣服

1991年2月

Spring Begins

Ah, here it is, the laughing spring is here
Prison is over

School ends in three days
The bird with hardened wings can now fly

Children are packing up
tracing the Long March with their hands

A child holds up a goat head and wails
He is crying for summer clothes

February 1991

家人

生活就是在家里吃饭
其中一个人开口了
他说："我是歌德
不是吃饭。"

他的妻子世态炎凉
感伤地坐在身边

接着是……
接着是为了歌德之事干杯
应表示尊重
这里还坐着一位尴尬的体育教师

请不要再叫我吃饭
请封口、封酒
当乡下人急急忙忙来到北京
做起了扣子生意

他妻子正世态炎凉
感伤地坐在身边

1991年2月

116

Family

Life is about dining at home
Someone opens his mouth
and says, *I'm Goethe*
I don't eat

His fickle wife
sits sadly by his side

Next . . .
A toast to Goethe
to show respect
An embarrassed sports teacher is also present

Please don't ask me to eat anymore
Shut up and stop drinking
Act like a peasant who runs to Beijing
to sell buttons

His fickle wife
sits sadly by his side

February 1991

除夕

墙上的无线电开口说话了
但请你不要对我说洞萧与兰草

如果此时我不在江苏
我也绝不会喝双沟酒

无话可说，无帽可脱
除夕，他只要求来一点水喝

写于1991年2月
改于2010年8月6日

New Year's Eve

The wireless radio starts to talk in the wall
But please don't say *flute* and *boneset*

If I'm not in Jiangsu right now
I'd certainly not drink Shuanggou wine

Not a word, not a hat
New Year's Eve, he just wants some water

February 1991
Revised August 6, 2010

衰老经

疲倦还疲倦得不够
人在过冬

一所房间外面
铁路黯淡的灯火，在远方

远方，远方人呕吐掉青春
并有趣地拿着绳子

啊，我得感谢你们
我认识了时光

但冬天并非替代短暂的夏日
但整整三周我陷在集体里

1991年4月

Scripture of Aging

Weary yet not weary enough
Man passes his winter

Outside a house
faint lights by the railroad, afar

afar, afar a man vomits up his youth
and playfully holds a rope

Ah, I must thank you all
I've known the passage of time

though winter can't replace brief summer days
though these three weeks I sink into the collective

April 1991

老诗人

阳春三月，田园善感
再过十天，他就五十岁了

他说还有一行诗在折磨他
哦，一颗扣子在折磨他

他头发潦草，像一个祖国
肥胖又一次激动桌面

文学，松松垮垮的文学
祖国，他视为业余的祖国

可他说：
文学应该因陋就简
祖国应该为此而出口

1991年2月

The Old Poet

March in the spring, pastoral sentiments
In ten days, he turns fifty

He says still one verse tortures him
No, it is a button torturing him

His hair in disarray, like a homeland
his fatness agitates the tabletop again

Literature, slack literature
Homeland, his amateur homeland

Yet he says:
Literature is simple because it is plain
This is why our homeland must export it

February 1991

(VII) *Hand Notes on Mountain and Water*

广陵散

一

一个青年向深渊滑去
接着又一个青年......

幸福就快报废了
一个男孩写下一行诗

唉，一行诗，只有一行诗
二十四桥明月夜

二

冬天的江南
令你思想散漫，抓不住主题

肴肉、个园、上海人
热气腾腾的导游者

照像吧，照像吧
他冻红的脸在笑

1993年2月

126

Ancient Tune of Guangling

1

A youth slides off toward the abyss
followed by another . . .

Bliss is soon outmoded
A boy writes a verse

Alas, a verse, just a verse
Twenty-four bridges in a moonlit night

2

Winter in the south
scatters your thoughts, they can't find a theme

Bacon, Geyuan Garden, Shanghai folks
a tour guide is steaming with enthusiasm

Photo, photo
His frozen red face is smiling

February 1993

棉花之歌

一日复一日，明日何其多
生活在一个工厂聚集
繁荣的棉花一股一股

工人们歌唱棉花
工人们购买棉花
工人们不出卖棉花

几何棉花、钞票棉花、爱情棉花
聚成中年叙事曲
集体主义锣鼓
肉体的平安夜
家家户户的欢乐

棉花是民生之歌
棉花是不失眠的
棉花是自力更生之母
当沿海城市升起了翅膀
棉花就抛弃海洋到大陆落户

哈哈大笑的棉花来了
哈哈大笑的一日三餐来了
哈哈大笑的工人阶级来了

一日复一日，明日何其多
生活在一个工厂聚集
繁荣的棉花一股一股

1994 春

Song of Cotton

Day after day, how many tomorrows
A factory life assembles
heaps and heaps of flourishing cotton

Workers sing cotton
Workers buy cotton
Workers do not betray cotton

Cotton geometry, cotton dollar notes, cotton love
clustered into narratives of middle-age
the drums of collectivism
the silent night of flesh
the joy of every family

Cotton is the people's song
Cotton is not an insomniac
Cotton is the mother of self-reliance
When the sea city lifts its wings
cotton will jilt the sea for the mainland

The laughing cotton is here
Three laughing meals are here
The laughing working class is here

Day after day, how many tomorrows
A factory life assembles
heaps and heaps of flourishing cotton

Spring 1994

山水手记

一

像原始人面对一个奇迹
我面对你的翻译和声音

二

毛泽东说：不要鹅蛋看不起鸡蛋。
枕草子说：水中的鸭蛋是优雅的。

三

年轻姑娘继续谈着风景，
一只燕子的飞翔会带来肉体的潮湿。

四

他有着黎明式的精神，但准时是他忧伤的表现。

五

鸟儿，
我心烦意乱
鸽子……
南京清晨的悸动

Hand Notes on Mountain and Water

1

Like a primitive facing a miracle
I face your translation and voice

2

Mao Tse-tung said, *Goose eggs should not look down on chicken eggs.*
The Pillow Book says, *Duck eggs in the water are elegant.*

3

The young girl continued to talk about the scenery,
the flight of a swallow could be sexually arousing.

4

He has a dawn-like spirit, but his punctuality expresses his sadness.

5

Bird,
I'm terribly distraught
Dove . . .
the pulse of an early Nanjing morning

六

风景有些寂寞的洋气
在一株皂角树下
凉风……
藤椅
一本五十年代的画册

七

他肠子里绞着算盘
他上演眼泪。

八

好听的地名是南京、汉城、名古屋。

九

年轻人烧指甲是会发疯的呀。

十

星期天，一个中年女教师
在无休止地打一条狗。

十一

我认为的好人是南京人吕祥，衢州人黄慰愿，合肥人胡全胜。

6

Some lonely foreign air in the landscape
under a Chinese honey locust
a fresh breeze . . .
the rattan chair
an art book from the fifties

7

His intestines are wrung with a Chinese abacus,
he performs tears.

8

Names of places that sound pleasant: Nanjing, Seoul and Nagoya.

9

Young people who burn their fingernails will go nuts.

10

On Sunday, a female teacher, middle-aged
beats a dog relentlessly.

11

I think good men include Lu Xiang from Nanjing, Huang Weiyuan
from Quzhou and Hu Quansheng from Hefei.

十二

爱流泪的胖子笑了，这一节值得留念。

十三

被焦虑损坏的脸是叶利钦的脸。

十四

这是春天的桌子，春天的椅子，春天的酒。

十五

一个深夜爱说话的体育教师今天专程去加拿大的月亮下哭泣。

十六

姓名叫杨伟的人不好，
应该改一个名字。

十七

一个美丽的男诗人发胖了，这是可悲的，他蓄上胡子就显得可爱了；
另一个男诗人流着眼泪说谎，而且头发又稀疏，就显得可耻了。

12

The tearful fatty smiles, this moment, worth keeping in fond memory.

13

The face ruined by anxiety is Yeltsin's.

14

This is spring table, spring chair, spring wine.

15

A sports teacher who likes to talk late at night makes a special trip today to cry under the moon in Canada.

16

The name *Yang Wei* is not auspicious,
they should change it.

17

A handsome male poet puts on weight, how sad, but if he wears a beard he'd look adorable; another poet is telling lies with tears, his hair thin and scarce, so despicable.

十八

我曾写过一行"向笑开枪"，
这很古怪。

十九

一个吃乌梢蛇时表情严肃的人是无趣的，一个在初夏头发多油的人是色情的；爱抒情的人注定了是坏人，而坏人的嘴都长得不好看。

二十

最柔软的女人是贵州女人。

二十一

我认识一位中国诗人，走路
像子弹一样快。

二十二

金鱼，这个词适合这张脸。

二十三

在柏林
我生出了第一根白发
是为记。

18

Once I wrote a line, *Shoot at laughter*,
how strange.

19

A man who looks stern when eating a Zaocys snake isn't amusing; a man
whose hair is greasy in early summer is lustful; a lyrical man is bound to
be a bad person and the mouth of the bad always looks ugly.

20

The softest women are Guizhou women.

21

I know a Chinese poet who walks
as fast as a bullet.

22

Goldfish, this verb fits this face.

23

In Berlin
I grew the first strand of white hair
as a souvenir

二十四

更明亮的在泻下
更强硬的在泻下
我想到机械化的钢琴心

二十五

1997年，10月
从斯图加特到图宾根
买一张周末车票35马克
但一次可乘坐5人。

二十六

他用榔头砸蚂蚁。

二十七

那女仆人捡起两节狗屎尾随而去
那老头搓着两个核桃若搓着两个睾丸

1995-1997

24

What is shinier is cascading down
What is harder is cascading down
I think of a mechanical piano heart

25

October 1997
from Stuttgart to Tübingen
I bought a weekend bus ticket for 35 Deutschmarks
valid for five passengers in one trip

26

He smashes ants with a hammer.

27

That maid picks up and walks away with two pieces of dog shit.
That old man rubs two peaches like rubbing two testicles.

1995–1997

两个时代之小影

"1897年春天，
契诃夫的右肺尖钝化，
7月，俄罗斯思潮社的沙发上有臭虫。"

2000年春天，
一位闲人把飞机和鸟儿运回成都，
7月，他又把棕榈树种上屋顶。

2000 秋

A Short Film on Two Eras

In the spring of 1897
Chekhov's right lung suffered a hemorrhage
In July, worms grow in a sofa from the Society of Russian Thought

In the spring of 2000
an idle man transports a model plane and a caged bird back to Chengdu
In July, he replants a palm tree on his roof

Autumn 2000

在猿王洞

这里的岁月很凉快。
面对群山和森林
我48岁的思绪突然集中了片刻。

苍蝇，两三只，闲闲地飞着，
很清瘦，很干净。
孩子们朝它喂饼，
一位红色小姐在拍它。

此时，我注意到了一个人，
他渴望生活，
于是他喝了酒。

2004 夏

In the Ape King's Cave

Time feels cool here
Facing mountains and their forest
thoughts of my forty-eight years suddenly gather

Two, three flies flutter freely
very slim, clean
Children feed it biscuits
a red lady gives it a pat

At this moment, I notice a man
who yearns for life
and drinks wine

Summer 2004

橘树下

—— 读翟永明《青春无奈》中一节有感

橘子树遮住了阎莉的小屋
在小屋里，我们升火做饭
火苗抖动着昏黄
她顺手摘下隔院橘树中的两个橘子

晚饭后，我们来到院子的橘树下
张跃进唱起了黄歌
歌声漂浮，流过我们
小灯盏般的红橘也迎向年轻的微风

透过细密的橘叶，月亮
无声地遍洒幸福的白银
夜深沉，空山鸟语后
另一个世界已笼罩了梨花沟

2008年12月31日于成都

Under the Mandarin Tree

— after an excerpt from *Alas, Youth* by Zhai Yongming

The mandarin tree covers Yan Li's hut
In the hut, we start a fire to cook
A faint yellow trembles in the flame
Casually she plucks two mandarins from the tree

We gather under the tree after dinner
Zhang Yuejin sings an erotic song
His floating voice flows over us
Like little lamps, mandarins greet the young wind

Through the fine leaves, moonlight
silently blankets the blessed silver
Deep night, birds sing in an empty mountain
The valley of pear flowers finds another world

Chengdu, December 31, 2008

(VIII) *Character Sketches*

谢幕

年轻时，他喜欢张罗
常在下午或黄昏
为我们送来一些小道具
录像带、气味、怪书……

生活总是不停地涌出呀
玩着孩子般的杂耍。他大笑：
匿名就是平等吗？
我搞不懂这是什么意思。

如今，他已52岁了。
"唉，这只老鼠活了30年。"
他边写边从叹息中加速：
"让它死！让它死！"

"世界是一个舞台，
我青春已逝，现在已轮到你们。"
看，他又变了一个腔调
他那哭声让周围的人愤怒。

2010年6月13日

Curtain Call

When he was young, he liked to brag
often in the afternoon or at dusk
sending us props
video tapes, scents, strange books . . .

Life can't always come in a gush
toying with tricks like children
He laughs, *Is anonymity equality?*
I don't understand what this means

He is already fifty-two now
Sigh, this mouse has lived for thirty years
Writing and sighing, his pen quickens
Let it die! Let it die!

The world is a stage
My youth is gone, now your turn
Look, he has become a soliloquy
his weeping enraging others

June 13, 2010

嘉陵江畔

不要怕，这只是一面镜子
面对遥远的往昔——

那天，滚烫的梯坎望不到尽头
你锻炼、奔跑……
在江边，正午，或黄昏
无眠的喜悦呢！
你总闻到一股怒气冲冲的味道
磅礴不绝，又难以形容

有人从巨石边飞跃入水
有人于江中追逐着驳船

而我却在那里
见到了一位淹死的青年
他面部苍白、肿胀
身上没有毛
看上去让人感到羞耻
如一具女人的尸体

从此，我失去了性别
从此，我看每一个人都像死人

2010年7月25日

Jialing River

Don't be afraid, this is just a mirror
facing a distant past —

That day, on an endless flight of scalding steps
you were training, running . . .
by the river, afternoon or evening
the joy of insomnia
always an odor of anger
majestic yet beyond description

Someone leapt into the water from a huge rock
Someone was chasing a barge in the river

But I was there
and saw a drowned youth
His face was ashen and swollen
body hairless
like a female corpse
putting others to shame

I am sexless ever since
I see everyone as a dead man ever since

July 25, 2010

黄山二日

你连续两天在黄山
在生活年轻的日子里

一个诗人的身体受尽虐待
他甚至从风景中滚下来

喏，集权的两小时
令人晕厥的两小时

那首歌唱完它平淡的复杂性
而老年的园艺学绝不在黄山

写于1990年12月11日
改于2010年8月6日

Two Days in Huangshan

Two days in a row in Huangshan
you live the days of youth

A poet's body suffers from abuse
He even tumbles from the landscape

So — two hours of centralizing power
two languishing hours

The song has sung its plain complexity
but the horticulture of old age is never in Huangshan

December 11, 1990
Revised August 6, 2010

酝酿

黑暗中，飘摇的街灯
在变着什么稀奇的魔术？

一个孩子正惊愕地站立街头

对面的窗户开着
几个人影围拢昏暗的灯火
好像在争论什么

宁静被其中一个人的咳嗽惊醒
显得如此地紧迫

那孩子仍站在那里一动不动。

2010年8月6日（改旧稿）

Brewing

In the dark, street lights drift
What strange magic is it?

A child stands shocked in the street

Opposite windows open
A few shadows crowd around a dim light
as if fighting over something

Stillness awakened rudely by a cough
seems so urgent

The child is still standing there, frozen

Revised August 6, 2010

夏日小令

一

那园里一角，有一株柿子树
风吹过时
让他产生了一种寂灭之感。

唉，"夏天最后几个憔悴的日子，
漫长的林荫道，
白杨树、手风琴、苦闷的诗歌……"

而另一个人说：
就在这株树下，佛陀睡去。

管它呢，
读完这二页
我朝灯看去，只感到愉快。

夏夜悠悠
似没有尽头
她一直拨弄着一枚凉爽的圆形纽扣。

而另一个人还在说：
就在这株树下呀，佛陀睡去。

Summer Lyric

I

A persimmon tree in a garden corner
When wind passes
a perishable feeling grows

Sigh, *The last sallow days of summer*
long boulevards
white poplars, accordion, gloomy poems . . .

Someone says
Buddha dozes off right under this tree

Who cares
After reading the second page
I look to the lamp and feel joy

Summer night drifts
as if endless
She keeps fiddling with a cool round button

Someone is saying
Buddha dozes off right under this tree

二

掌灯时分，一缕青烟飘了上来
"鹤之眼"，你到底在看什么？

看那室内神经般颤抖的植物
正令她惊悚

看他在渐浓的夜色里打开灯
去书架上寻找一本书

是的，这时我也听到了
一颗易于激动的少年心

它像1966年夏日中午的一小节波浪
正流经重庆嘉陵江心之中央

对，那是一个幻觉
但，我在荡漾……

2010年8月6日

2

Holding a lamp, a wisp of green smoke rises
Eye of a crane, what are you looking at?

Look how an indoor plant that shivers nervously
thrills her

Look how he turns on a lamp in the thickening night
to search for a book on the shelf

Yes, I also hear
a young heart easily stirred

like a wave in a summer afternoon of 1966
flowing through the heart of Jialing River

Yes, that is an illusion
Still, I ripple . . .

August 6, 2010

风在说

睡觉的愿望就像一场追寻。
——赫塔·米勒

一

风儿，已躺下，
黑暗里，风之絮语比风本身还沉：

她在瘦下去，仅仅三天，
脸就有了一缕放陈的香梨味

树叶开始发黄，不远处
一股怀旧的锈铁迎面吹度

这时，我会想，
她的呢喃为何如缎被上的金鱼呢？

冰凉欲滴……
最后的"变形记"终被打开：

她"越不想活，就越爱化妆。"
越爱在平静中飞旋起她酒后的烦闷。

Wind Says

Sleep wish is like a search.
— Herta Müller

I

Wind has laid down
in the dark, the whisper of wind is denser than wind:

She is losing weight, in just three days
an old pear aroma graces her face

Leaves wither, not far away
a nostalgic gust of rusty iron blows

And I'd wonder
Why does she murmur like a goldfish embroidered on a satin quilt?

Icy drips . . .
The last of *The Metamorphosis* opens at last:

The more she doesn't speak, the more she loves cosmetics
the more she calmly spins her woes after wine

二

睡下的风，继续讲着另一个故事
它在轻叩我的不安：

35年过去了，那卧病多年的父亲
已在风景中死去；
乡间，在竹林中，
那丧父的儿子也垂垂老矣，
我从此痛失我的知青岁月

——深冬，绝对的午后
腊猪头在灶膛里已煨了一昼夜
那虚胖的儿子请我去吃，
是的，吃！我记得：
"这一天，天空比一只眼睛还要小。"
这一天，你的请吃声恍若大唐之音

三

风从深夜起身，开始哈气，
第三个故事由情（不自禁地）说出：

早年，61岁的花花公子何来悲伤，
脸上总溢满社会主义右派的笑容；
骑着妖娆的自行车，他常常
一溜烟就登上南京卫岗的陡坡

如今他已痴呆，整天裹一件睡衣，
裸着下体在室内晃荡，
他浪漫的妻子受不了他的臭味
以及他外表的苍老和内心的幼稚

2

Wind in sleep continues another story
It knocks softly on my disquiet:

Thirty-five years have passed, a father who was ill for many years
passed away in this landscape
Countryside, in bamboo forests
the mourning son is also aging
I have since lost my years of educated youth

— Late winter, in a perfect afternoon
a cured pig head simmering overnight on the stove
The puffy son invited me over
Yes, eat! I remember:
This day, the sky is smaller than an eye
This day, your invitation struck like Tang music

3

Wind gets up from late night, and starts to exhale
The third story (can't help but) begin(s) from romance:

In his early years, the playboy now sixty-one had no sorrows
His face was always full of right-winged socialist smiles
Riding an enchanted bike, he took
the Nanjing Weigang slope in a dash

Senile, he wrapped himself in pyjamas all day long
swaying indoors with a naked lower body
His romantic wife could not bear his stench
his old appearance and childish mind

终于，他最后的时刻到了，
睁眼睡入军区医院的病床；
戴上呼吸机，开始分秒必争的长跑
整整三个月，他似一个初学呼吸的人类，

不停地跑呀，不能停下，停下就是死亡。
很快，岁月在他那曾经灿烂的屌上枯谢了
很快，岁月走过的地方，都轻轻撒一点
他独有的尿味、皮肤味、香水味

2011年1月27日

When his time arrived at last
he landed wide-eyed in a military hospital bed
wearing a respirator, beginning a marathon
For three months, he was like a man learning to breathe

running non-stop, couldn't stop, to stop was to die
Soon, years withered his once glorious cock
Soon, places visited by years were sprinkled with
the unique odor of his urine, skin, and perfume

January 27, 2011

人物速记

一

端着那不自知的发奋之姿
他学习写作，
日日夜夜不苟言笑
一如南方来的冰冻之客。

垂暮之夜酒、沉默之水果
以及花生
通通被他吃掉
一如粮食喂养着一具未来的尸体。

二

她递给我一枚指甲，我将其擦亮
那指甲边缘有光

我会消逝。
但鱼化石；
但"一些瞬间的我也许会在她的身上继续生存。"

三

那少年在一碧幽潭里见识了晚春的深夜
现在，他在四川省军区操场上
无限地、无限地……
拨弄着一辆自行车上永恒的铃铛。

166

Character Sketches

1

In a pose of unconscious drive
he learns to write
seriously, day and night
like a frozen guest from the south

Aging night wine, silent fruits
and peanuts
all eaten up
like food that feeds a future corpse

2

She gave me a fingernail, I polished it
Its edge shone

I will fade away
But fish melts into stone
Some instants of me might keep on living in her

3

The youth learned about late spring nights by a secluded lake
Now he is in a military playground in Sichuan
infinitely, infinitely . . .
fiddling with an eternal bell on a bike

四

在柏林，Kumiko 家的花园里
我见识了一地嫩绿的核桃
那天下午，凉气感人、室内安静
我们畅谈着生活……
从一册书里，我们甚至找到了
日语中的白居易

突然，她老年的眼光美极了
正迎向今后岁月的某个人；
突然，天色转暗、寒风叩窗
一位年轻的注定的神呵
——为我们带来了朗读
带来了更多的风景与前程……

五

深夜的沙发刚刚睡去，摸一摸
上面还有才离开的客人的余温
室内烟雾缭绕，残茶冷却，
他提走了一袋瘦词、一袋失眠的思想

在南方，春寒冻坏了我的食指
清晨，听春燕呢喃吗？
不。最初的燕子是阴郁的。
那就孤独地吃完早餐
孤独地坐在电脑前开始一天的工作

2010年12月19日－2011年1月6日

168

4

In Berlin, in Kumiko's garden
I learned about a vivid green world of walnuts
That afternoon, it was cool and moving, and quiet inside
We chatted about life . . .
In a book, we even found
the Japanese Po Chü-I

Suddenly, her old eyes turned so lovely
greeting someone from future years
Suddenly, the sky turned dark, cold wind knocked on the window
Ah, a doomed young god
— to present us a recital
to present us landscapes and future . . .

5

On a sofa late at night I barely fell asleep, touching
the warmth from a guest who'd just left
Misty smoke spiraled in the house, cold tea remained
He took away a bag of thin verbs, a bag of sleepless thoughts

In the south, spring chill freezes my forefinger
Early morning, can you hear the soft chirping of swallows?
No. Early swallows are sullen
So finish breakfast alone
Sit before the computer and start work alone

December 19, 2010 – January 6, 2011

小学生活

那孩子的心呀在课堂上漫游
累了，他的身体就想动
"到办公室去！"
老师已提前发出了命令
那孩子被罚站一个下午

黄昏星升起，放学的龙卷风
刮过大田湾小学的石阶
那孩子的面孔变了，
他开始死盯一株树或仰望夜空
或蜷缩在公共汽车上期待入眠

痛苦中断，也无惊疯
那孩子只在羡慕中久久地出神：
当家长与亲戚们吃完明亮的晚餐
他也一觉醒来，长大成人。

2011年1月6日

Primary School Life

The boy's mind is roaming in class
Tired, his body will fidget
Go to the office!
The teacher has already issued his order
The punished boy stands for an afternoon

A dusky star rises, an after-school tornado
sweeps past the stone steps of Datianwan Primary School
The boy's face changes
He starts to stare at a tree, to gaze at the night sky
to cuddle in a public car awaiting sleep

Misery breaks down, yet no hysteria
The boy just loses himself to thoughts in envy:
when parents and kin finish their bright dinner
he too wakes up, and grows up

January 6, 2011

西藏书

无常（二）

阅读这本书时，
室内的光线已变暗。这一页翻过，

我开始幻想尼泊尔寺院上空的秋云……
如此短暂；
我那微细的毛发呀，它在变。
那些卑贱的人或高贵的人终将死去……

记忆——

急流冲泄、一滑而过

一位身材高大的上师在那里讲经。

2010年11月22日

from The Book of Tibet

Impermanence (II)

Reading this book
light dims in the room, turning this page over

I imagine an autumn cloud over a temple in Nepal . . .
so transient
my faint body hair is evolving
those lowly or lofty men will die someday . . .

Memory —

It slides away in a torrent

A towering guru is giving a sermon

November 22, 2010

逝去，逝去……

天空迎面扑来，初冬宛如初夏
黄昏里，那幢楼房、那间病室

她
无法以一颗欢乐心进入哀歌

她日里问夜里问，每隔一会儿都要问：
我死时会是什么样子呢？

凡心是风口的灯火，无法稳定
困难——超过那只浮在水面的乌龟

注意：
一只小昆虫正把你的小手指看成伟大的山水呢

逝去，逝去……
让我们的心在寺院。

2010年11月29日

Fading, Fading . . .

Sky greets us, early winter, early summer
at dusk, that building, that ward

She
can't put a joyful heart in an elegy

She asks day and night, from time to time:
How would I look when I die?

A worldly heart is a lantern in a wind gap, unstable
in adversity — more than a turtle floating on water

Note:
a tiny insect sees your finger as a vast landscape

Fading, fading . . .
let our hearts stay in the temple

November 29, 2010

吐蕃男子

吐蕃男子持铁，
下颌长出毛就用钳子拔去。
吐蕃男子不弃，
用死去父母的头颅做成钵和杯子。

（而巫师吃人肉，召唤好天气；
而祭师切尸体，引来天空的神鹰）

某个吐蕃男子有狭长的仪表——
一月弯刀；
某个吐蕃男子风马凌空
不重
恍如掠过水面的燕子……

2010年12月3日

176

The Tibetan

the Tibetan is holding iron
when his underjaw grows hair he pulls it out with pliers
the Tibetan does not give up
uses his parents' skulls for earthern bowls and cups

(the sorcerer eats human flesh, summons good weather
the priest cuts a corpse, lures condors from the sky)

a certain Tibetan has a long, narrow look —
a moon a sickle
a certain Tibetan soars like a wind horse
light
like a swallow skimming over water . . .

December 3, 2010

Notes

I
"Precipice"

Diao Chan was one of the four ancient beauties of China. She appears as a fictional character in the historical novel, *Romance of the Three Kingdoms*.

Li Ho (791–817) was a Tang poet known for his mystical writings.

III
"Emperor Li Yu"

Also known as Li Houzhu, Emperor Li Yu (937–978) was the last reigning ruler (961–975) of the Southern Tang Kingdom during the era of Five Dynasties and Ten Kingdoms. A fine poet, he was a master of *ci*, a classical form of Chinese lyrical poetry.

IV
"To Osip Mandelstam"

Born in Warsaw, Russian poet and essayist Osip Mandelstam (1891–1938) was raised in St. Petersburg. He first published his poems in the journal *Apollyon* in 1910. During the Silver Age, he formed with Anna Akhmatova, Nikolai Gumilev and Sergei Gorodetsky the Acmeist school of poets (or the Guild of Poets). After reciting to his friends an epigram denouncing Stalin ("the huge laughing cockroaches on his top lip") in 1934, he was arrested and sent to exile. He died four years later in a transit camp in the Gulag, near Vladivostok.

"Jonestown"

Jonestown is a former settlement in North Guyana, South America and the site of an American religious cult called "The People's Temple," which was founded in 1955 by Indianapolis preacher, James Warren Jones. On November 18, 1978, 914 people died in a mass suicide in Jonestown and a nearby airstrip, as well as in Georgestown (the Temple's headquarters and capital of Guyana).

V
"Wheat: In Memory of Hai Zi"

Considered a major Chinese poetic voice, Hai Zi (1964–1989) has a posthumous cult-like status in China. Born and raised in a farming village in Anhui Province, he passed the entrance exam to the prestigious Beijing University at fifteen. At twenty, he started teaching philosophy and art theory at China University of Political Science and Law. During his brief yet explosive life, he wrote about 250 poems and several epics, portraying an intense mix of illuminating yet complex visions of his difficult society. Hai Zi remained poor throughout his life, and committed suicide in 1989 by laying himself on a railroad track at Beijing Shanhaiguan. He was twenty-five.

VI
"Reality"

Lu Xun (1881–1936) and Lin Yutang (1895–1976) are considered as two most influential Chinese writers of the twentieth century who championed modernism in Chinese literature. Lu Xun saw literature as a way of spiritual and political awakening, while Lin Yutang was a pioneer in promoting bilingualism and translation in English and Chinese.

VIII

"Wind Says"

The "years of educated youth" refer to the years of 1975 till 1978, when Bai Hua was sent to the countryside in Ba County, Chongqing for labor and political reform as an educated youth.

"The Tibetan"

The image "a wind horse" also implies a prayer flag.

The Enigma of Time, Cities and Voices

Fiona Sze-Lorrain: Places and seasons play an integral role in your poetry, both lyrically and theatrically. I think of Nanjing, Chongqing, and summer, for example. How do you reconcile, revisit and reinvigorate time and space as compositional elements in your poetic creation?

Bai Hua: Time has always been the greatest wonder for me. Why is it now, but not then? Why did he die, while she was born? "And those weeping," and "a sound from moving water". . . I had poured out all of these in "Expression," a poem I wrote in October 1981 in Guangzhou. Why would I suddenly put down my pen (and stop writing poetry) for fifteen years, and then suddenly begin to write anew in 2007? This mystery is closely associated with time: it makes me ponder, but without explanation. Yet it is often the miracle of time that summons me, luring me closely behind it. I write, I stop, I write again . . .

What makes me shiver most in terms of time is summer. Yes, once I open my mouth and say "summer," no matter when and where, my voice will enter an inexplicable lyricism. "Summer" is a concept of time in my poetry. It is the most glorious season, yet it is also the beginning of the season of withering. It contains the fine but complicated understandings I have of life. I consider "summer" both as a noun and a verb. Through this word, I express my lamentations toward life, and in particular life in Jiangnan. You can say that without summer, I wouldn't have begun writing poetry. Summer is me, I am summer. Just as wheat is Hai Zi, Hai Zi is wheat.

As for those destined places — Chongqing, my place of birth (the most unique city in China, which I evoke in an essay from my book of nonfiction, *On the Left: A Lyrical Poet from the Mao Era*); Nanjing, my place of wanderings; Guangzhou, where I studied; Chengdu, my place of residence — the fact that they have crossed paths with different years of my life transforms itself into an unfathomable yet inexhaustible source of theatricality. I lived in Chongqing till I turned twenty-one, after which thirty years of migration and wandering followed. Despite the fact that I despise my overly intense Chongqing soul, that city has never left me. Among the four cities, I love Nanjing most. Cities exert an undeniable influence on any writing life, and that is the case for these four cities and me. I constantly strive to do my very best in poetry — an art of memory — so that it can shine in my life, and console the fading past, and retain what is about to fade away.

You know, every place I visit, every repetitive detail in each season is always so significant, that I must do my utmost to speak of its various mysteries and beauty. I also possess a kind of foresight. For example, when I visit a certain site, I immediately get a sense if it would one day become an unforgettable poem of memory.

How has your relationship with poetry evolved since your poetic silence of over a decade?

I have become much more broad-minded. My ways of entering poetry have diversified; they are richer, I am more self-confident and poised. I have finally understood: other than in my young but nervous imagination, poetry can be found in the market, factory, toilets or by the bedside. This is why I am now writing the series "Historical Annals," and do not care about the hatred, rage, criticism and mockery some young people have shown toward such a writing style.

During my poetic silence, I did not have the fear of not being able to write. To borrow the words of Baudelaire, "Men are weary of writing, women are weary of romance." Silence is not empty. Let the silence be — a poetic silence is also something worth celebrating, so why fear?

In your most recent sequenced poems — such as "The Book of Tibet," "Gift" and "Notes from the Late Qing" — that hybridize prose with verse, as well as different voices, musicalities and narratives, you employ various linguistic registers. How do you relate to such a multi-layered poetic structure, its emotional responses and interpretation?

When I was young, I had already come up with this poetic ideal of "weaving prose with poetry," that is, "all mingled in one," mingling all linguistic genres into one melting pot. When I began to write "An Immortal Companion to Watercolor" and "Historical Annals," I started to find ways to hybridize the novel, prose, theatre, and even journalism with poetry, and to achieve this intertextuality with skill and ease. Of course, such techniques are not original. Experiments with sound, voice and presence define much of contemporary and avant-garde poetics. As to how I would blend all of these voices into a melting pot, I, too, don't quite know. I just do so with a little common sense, and let the technique function as it best can.

Do you see a poem as an experience or as an act?

One can't be separated from the other "Poetry is experience" — this is a universally-known dictum from the German poet, Rilke. Even Nabokov who detested Rilke, also said, "Poetry is a distant past." But poetry must also be an act in a modern sense, and even more so in a post-modern context. If I must choose between the two of them, an old poet like me would go for the former.

Ezra Pound says, "Make it new." You have a skillful way of making the language both "new" and "fresh" when it comes to developing a unique signature in Chinese in terms of the language as a tradition, but without the antecedents of a so-called "modern" poetry or the preconceived "traditional." In "A Year of Chronicler in Suzhou" and "In the Qing Dynasty," for instance, the ancient idioms (成语,

proverbs (俗语) and sayings (惯用语) are able to express intention: they speak and show without telling.

As a contemporary poet, how do you engage with the "tradition" during the interior process of writing? As a contemporary reader, how do you approach the so-called classical Chinese poetry?

My understanding and approach toward tradition draws its influence from the celebrated essay of T.S. Eliot, "Tradition and the Individual Talent." Personally, I don't have any new perspective or unusual rhetoric to offer regarding "tradition." To put it more plainly, reading Chinese classical poetry, for a contemporary reader, is to foster one's *qi*. It is a way of literary self-cultivation through reading choices and learning of oneself.

So how do/should we read them? Obviously I am thinking of Eliot's famous saying, "Immature poets imitate, great poets steal." Or as Vladimir Nabokov once said, "Only true geniuses will take things from others to use as their own." Work that can be stolen or "taken to be used" is never first-rate work. However, these less than first-rate writings are able to survive (survival being their best fate) because they are waiting to be read by a certain great poet, to be taken away again.

To take a step further, many writings by second-rate poets or soon-to-be-first-rate poets are often destined to be "stolen" by another strong poet. The former exists only for the latter. After which, the former "dies," for its mission is over. Does that mean that a great poet would steal everywhere? No. Certainly there are limits. As I have previously mentioned, great poets will only steal from second-rate or soon-to-be-first-rate poets. If they meet another true poet, no matter how they would like to steal, they cannot. Even if they can, it is useless. They will end up as mere imitators. Let me also quote another thought-provoking saying, "Learn from the living Eileen Chang, and the dead Hu Lancheng." ("学张爱玲生, 学胡兰成死")

How do you feel about poetry that may appear to disavow communication, show-ing more apparent interest in pursuing "aesthetics"?

The latter is the intrinsic nature of poetry. The poetry I pursue is subtle and shuddering. It reveals the mystery of life and death, and never opens itself up to sluggish people. I go for swiftness, intensity and events in my poems. Poetry isn't simply mathematics. It is the enigmatic calculus — po-etry is not a mathematical form of communication, but the transforma-tional beauty of geometry.

How would you describe the speaker(s) in your own poems?

According to conventional principles in contemporary poetry, I am the di-rector of each poem. I will direct every character in each *mise en scène* ac-cording to each narrative. Thus, the speaker in my poems will also change accordingly, playing different roles with different pronoun references. In *The Three Voices of Poetry*, T.S. Eliot defines the three voices of poetry in the following manner:

> The first is the voice of the poet talking to himself — or to nobody. The second is the voice of the poet addressing an audience, whether large or small. The third is the voice of the poet when he attempts to create a dramatic character speaking in verse; when he is saying, not what he would say in his own person, but only what he can say within the limits of one imaginary character addressing another imaginary character.[1]

This is also my approach toward the "speaker" in my own poems.

---

1. Eliot, T.S. *The Three Voices of Poetry*. New York: Cambridge University Press, 1954. 6–7.

You are widely known as a lyrical poet, and have claimed the mysterious and the inexplicable as a vital presence in poetry. Do you feel that emotional honesty should and can be compromised for ambiguity?

I have mixed feelings about this question. Can sincere honesty be compromised by ambiguity? I can't help but think of Ezra Pound, "Technique is the test of sincerity." I believe as long as a poet masters his poetic techniques well, his emotional honesty will not be compromised by expression. A truly good poem will contain both emotional honesty and technical mastery. Let us also revisit Baudelaire's poem, *"Le Balcon,"* which was discussed in detail by T.S. Eliot in his essay on the French poet:

> In *"Le Balcon,"* which M. Valéry considers, and I think rightly, one of Baudelaire's most beautiful poems, there is all the romantic idea, but something more: the reaching out towards something which cannot be had *in,* but which may be had partly *through,* personal relations. Indeed, in much romantic poetry the sadness is due to the exploitation of the fact that no human relations are adequate to human desires, but also to the disbelief in any further object for human desires than that which, being human, fails to satisfy them.[2]

As a representative figure of the post-"Misty" poets, what are your thoughts about the tides of poetry and artistic search in the present-day China?

When a tide is over, one will become a tradition. When one becomes a tradition, he or she will also open up a new tide. This dialectic simply means: the more you pursue the art that impassions you, the more you will find yourself right at the source of a tide.

---

2. Eliot, T.S. *Selected Prose of T.S. Eliot.* Ed. Frank Kermode. New York: Harcourt Inc., 1975. 235.

In some ways, I consider myself as part of the transitional tide between "Misty" and post-"Misty" poetry movements.

As a contemporary Chinese poet, to what extent does the question or issue of a readership stand as an agenda for you?

Of course, the more readers there are, the better it is. We can sell more poetry books. But the fate of contemporary poetry has already determined its very small scope of readership. Contemporary poetry is aimed at those who suffer or are ill in their inner lives. Let me make a bold guess: these are — very possibly — men who are overly feminine and women who are overly masculine.

The question of gendering in poetics — particularly in a masculine broth such as the contemporary Chinese poetry scene — can be a delicate and complex issue. How does the poet's gender politicize his or her work?

It will be quite an effort for me to explain my thoughts about "men who are overly feminine and women who are overly masculine"… Life always carries a pure yearning that resists death. Poetry begins from this intense yearning. Its value is defined by the lofty yet irreplaceable luxury of ideals; it nourishes highly neuropathic but beautiful souls.

In general, I am a little dubious as to whether the real masculine sex can truly and fully understand poetry, though I have never doubted if women or men with feminine qualities can do so (Most male poets possess feminine traits. Brodsky once said, "I am even more feminine than Tsvetaeva.") Coupled with their solitude, idleness, frailness and sensitivities, women indulge naturally in poetry.

Do you have an ideal reader?

By chance you may meet this reader, but he or she cannot be sought. If you allow a most honest answer from me: my ideal reader can only be myself. So, to reveal something that is not quite proper in terms of public relations: I usually only read my poems. In fact, I read all of them again and again, to the extent that I almost do not read others' work.

How do you nourish your poetic life?

Read, read, read. Non-stop. In a jumble, in chaos.

Right now I am reading Herta Müller, as well as my favorites, Wu Wen-ying and Vladimir Nabokov. It is very difficult for me to cite a specific list of reading indispensables. In the past, whenever someone had asked me to come up with a list of "must-reads," I would do so spontaneously. But, after some time, I would always feel that something was not quite right, as if these titles themselves were letting out an inexplicable sense of regret or lamentation once they landed on a sheet of white paper.

Being such a voracious reader, do you also see other "non-literary" possibilities as your artistic influences? If so, what are they?

I have never really thought about this, but now that you mention it, I did think about an influence that is not literary-related — music. Often, I finish some of my poems while listening to a melody or while singing. Some simple and lyrical music as long as it can stimulate my thoughts. Sometimes films excite me, too. For example, Andrei Tarkovsky's *Mirror* (1975) had directly inspired me to write a stanza in my poem, "Gift":

In the heavy rain, she opened the iron door of the press
rushing into the layout room of socialism, verifying
an original phrase from Chekhov's *Collected Works*. Perhaps
sparrows fly by the window dotted with rust stains.

*Beyond writing, what is meaningful in life for you? How would you like to reach
out toward a wider humanity?*

First and foremost, family is particularly important to me. Four seasons
and a life — thoughts or poetry at different moments in time is never the
same. Only difference can widen one's thoughts or poetry. For instance,
when gazing at the sky at a young age, you might easily recite John Keats,
"When I have fears that I may cease to be." In years to come, you may
instead evoke Confucius' "Could one but go on and on like this, never
ceasing day or night!"

Age changes you, like river moved by its own flow will widen its river bed.
According to Confucius, "At seventy, I could follow the dictates of my own
heart; for what I desired no longer overstepped the boundaries of right."
On the other hand, Jorge Luis Borges says in one of his lectures at Harvard,
"This Craft of Verse," "I hope I can attain real happiness when I reach the
ripe age of sixty-seven."

*Originally conducted in Chinese in June/July 2010, this interview was translated by
Fiona Sze-Lorrain, who edited and adapted it with Sally Molini. An abridged version
has also appeared in* Cerise Press.

JINTIAN SERIES OF CONTEMPORARY LITERATURE

In Print

Flash Cards
Yu Jian
Translated by Wang Ping & Ron Padgett

The Changing Room
Zhai Yongming
Translated by Andrea Lingenfelter

Doubled Shadows
Ouyang Jianghe
Translated by Austin Woerner

A Phone Call from Dalian
Han Dong
Edited by Nicky Harman
Translated by Nicky Harman, Maghiel van Crevel,
Yu Yan Chen, Naikan Tao, Tony Prince & Michael Day

Forthcoming

I Can Almost See the Clouds of Dust
Yu Xiang
Translated by Fiona Sze-Lorrain

October Dedications
Mang Ke
Edited by Lucas Klein
Translated by Lucas Klein, Huang Yibing
and Jonathan Stalling